MW01233995

Maya Angelou

Corinne J. Naden and Rose Blue

Raintree

Chicago, Illinois

Photo research by Bill Broyles

Printed and bound in China by South China Printing Company.
10 09 08 07 06
10 9 8 7 6 5 4 3 2 1

Library of Congress Cataloging-in-Publication Data:

Naden, Corinne J.
  Maya Angelou / Corinne J. Naden and Rose Blue.
    p. cm. -- (African-American biographies)
  Includes bibliographical references and index.
  ISBN 1-4109-1042-3 (hc) 1-4109-1119-5 (pb)
 1. Angelou, Maya--Juvenile literature. 2. Authors, American--20th century--Biography--Juvenile literature. 3. African American authors--Biography--Juvenile literature. I. Blue, Rose. II. Title. III. Series: African American biographies (Chicago, Ill.)
  PS3551.N464Z797 2005
  818'.5409--dc22

                    2005004826

Acknowledgments
The publisher would like to thank the following for permission to reproduce photographs:
p. 4 Christopher Felver/Corbis; pp. 8, 34, 43 courtesy Dr. Maya Angelou; p. 11 Corbis; p. 13 Arkansas State Library; pp. 18, 22, 36, 38, 41, 44, 48 Bettmann/Corbis; p. 20 Labor Archives and Research Center, San Francisco State University; p. 25 Underwood & Underwood/Corbis; p. 26 Photofest; p. 29 Morton Beebe/Corbis; p. 31 George Karger/Pix Inc./Time Life Pictures/Getty Images; p. 46 Burt Shavitz/Pix Inc./Time Life Pictures/Getty Images; p. 50 A. Ramey/Photo Edit; p. 52 AP Wide World Photo; p. 54 Columbia/The Kobal Collection/Picture Desk; p. 56 Leif Skoogfors/Corbis; p. 59 Los Angeles Times photo/ABACA Press

Cover photograph: Los Angeles Times photo/ABACA Press

Every effort has been made to contact copyright holders of any material reproduced in this book. Any omissions will be rectified in subsequent printings if notice is given to the publisher

Some words are shown in bold, **like this.** You can find out what they mean by looking in the Glossary.

Contents

Maya Angelou is shown here in a publicity photo in 1984. The same year, Angelou received an honorary degree from Winston-Salem State University in North Carolina. Honorary degrees are awards of recognition given by colleges and universities.

Introduction:
The Heart of a Woman

S he is a poet and author. She is a **playwright**. She is an actress, producer, and director. She is a singer and dancer and a teacher and speaker. She is a **civil rights activist**. She is a mother and grandmother. But most of all, she is a survivor. She has survived abuse and **racism**. She has survived poverty and sadness. She is Maya Angelou, one of the great voices of American literature.

Growing up in a small town in Arkansas, Maya Angelou learned about poverty and racism at a very early age. People often thought less of her because of the color of her skin. It took many years before she learned to be proud of her heritage. It took many more years before she had enough self-confidence to use her gifts.

Today, Maya Angelou is known and respected around the world. Her books and poems are read by millions. She has entertained children and has been celebrated by presidents. Most of her work

In Her Own Words

What **discrimination** and **racism** can do to the heart of a young girl is shown clearly in these words by Maya Angelou as she describes listening to a white speaker, Edward Donleavy, at her eighth-grade graduation.

". . . Donleavy had exposed us. We were maids and farmers, handymen and washerwomen. . . . It was awful to be Negro and have no control over my life. It was brutal to be young and already trained to sit quietly and listen to charges brought against my color with no chance of defense. We should all be dead. I thought I should like to see us all dead, one on top of the other. . . .

My name had lost its ring of familiarity and I had to be nudged to go up and receive my diploma. All my preparations had fled. I neither marched up to the stage like a conquering Amazon, nor did I look in the audience for Bailey's nod of approval. Marguerite Johnson, I heard the name again, my honors were read, there noises in the audience of appreciation, and I took my place on the stage as rehearsed. I thought about colors I hated: ecru, puce, lavender, beige, and black."

From *I Know Why the Caged Bird Sings*

is about growing up as a African-American child in the United States and about how she feels about being an African American today.

Maya Angelou also writes and speaks about the challenges all people face, no matter what their backgrounds. In an interview printed in *Smithsonian* magazine in April 2003, she said that no matter how bad things seem, "somehow morning comes, and we get up and continue on."

Angelou is seen in this family photo when she was fifteen and attending high school.

Chapter 1:
Lessons of Childhood

Marguerite Annie Johnson was born on April 4, 1928, in St. Louis, Missouri. She did not take the name Maya Angelou until the 1950s. Her brother, Bailey, called her "My," which later became "Maya." Her family called her "Ritie," short for Marguerite.

The Johnson family moved to Long Beach, California, when Marguerite was still an infant. In 1931 her parents divorced. Marguerite and Bailey went to live with their father's mother, Annie Henderson, and their uncle, Willie, in Stamps, Arkansas. With handwritten tags tied to their wrists that read "To Whom It May Concern," Marguerite and Bailey traveled to Arkansas alone by train. Other passengers looked after them and gave them food. Bailey was four and Marguerite was only three.

Marguerite's grandmother—called "Momma" by Marguerite—was a clever woman. Many years before, Momma's husband left her alone to care for their young sons (one of whom would grow up to become Marguerite's father). Momma had to find a way to make enough money to care for herself and children. She was a good cook, so she made fried meat pies and sold them to the men working at the local lumber mill and cotton gin. In a few years, she made enough money to open a store where she could sell her pies. She later turned the small pie shop into a general store where people could shop for many different things. By the time Marguerite came to live with Momma, the store was also a place where people gathered to talk and share news.

Most of Momma's customers came early in the morning on their way to work. Marguerite and Bailey rose at dawn to serve the customers. Many of them worked long, hard days picking cotton for very little pay. In the evenings, they came back to the store looking beaten down and tired. Seeing them day after day made Marguerite realize how difficult it was to be poor.

Stamps, Arkansas, was a difficult town for African-American people to live in. It was extremely **segregated** and black people lived in a part of town that was much poorer than the area where white people lived. Marguerite and Bailey sometimes had to travel into the white part of town to buy fresh meat to eat. This always filled Marguerite with fear. She had heard stories about the Ku Klux

When Marguerite was growing up in the South, African Americans often had physically demanding farm jobs. The woman pictured is shown picking cotton in Arkansas in 1938.

The Ku Klux Klan

In 1866 former Southern Civil War veterans in Tennessee formed the Ku Klux Klan. The Klan started as a social club, but soon its members began harassing and sometimes even killing African Americans. In 1868 the Klan killed nearly 1,000 people in Louisiana alone. In the 1920s, when more and more **immigrants** were coming to the United States, the Klan became popular again. They elected their members to political offices and enforced **segregation** in some parts of the South. The Klan continues to exist today, although it is not as powerful as it once was.

Klan, a group of white men who terrorized African Americans and sometimes killed them. In spite of this fear, Marguerite felt loved and protected by her grandmother while she lived in Stamps.

She also comforted herself by turning to books. Marguerite and Bailey attended the Lafayette County Training School where she studied hard. She especially enjoyed reading books by Edgar Allen Poe, William Shakespeare, and African-American poet Langston Hughes. Once, when Marguerite and Bailey wanted to perform a piece of literature for Momma, they chose some lines for a play by Shakespeare. But they soon changed their minds and memorized a poem by James Weldon Johnson, an African-American

This photo shows the lumberyards of a business in Stamps, Arkansas, that produced paper around the same time that Marguerite was growing up there.

writer, instead. They were afraid Momma would disapprove of William Shakespeare because he was white.

Back to St. Louis

For the five years they were in Stamps, Marguerite and Bailey did not hear from their parents, except for getting Christmas gifts from them one year. Then, when Marguerite was seven, her father showed up in Stamps and announced that he was taking Marguerite and Bailey back to St. Louis. Marguerite did not want to go, but she had no choice.

Shortly after they arrived in St. Louis, Marguerite's father left her and Bailey with their mother and her boyfriend, Mr. Freeman. At first, Mr. Freeman seemed harmless, but not long after Marguerite and Bailey moved in, he began to abuse Marguerite. Mr. Freeman threatened to kill Bailey if she told anyone about the abuse. Marguerite kept quiet, creating a safe world for herself in her imagination. Eventually, Bailey and her mother discovered the truth, and Mr. Freeman was arrested.

Silence

At Freeman's trial, Marguerite had to tell her version of what Freeman had done to her. Freeman was found guilty and sentenced to a year in jail, but he was later released without serving his full time. A few days after the trial, his body was found in an alley. He had been kicked to death.

Marguerite was horrified. She thought her testimony was the reason he had been killed. Now she thought she was cursed. What if she spoke and made someone else die? She decided not to speak to anyone but Bailey and was silent for almost five years. Not knowing how to help her daughter, Marguerite's mother sent her and Bailey back to Stamps, Arkansas.

A year after moving back to Stamps, Marguerite met Bertha Flowers, a friend of Momma's. She was the most sophisticated African-American woman Marguerite had ever met. Bertha encouraged Marguerite's love of reading, but also taught her the importance of using her voice. She gave Marguerite books to read and pushed her to read them out loud. In this way, Marguerite gained the confidence to speak again.

On the move again

In 1940, when Marguerite was twelve years old, she was excited about graduating from eighth grade. She was one of the best students in her class, and she felt the whole world was out there for her to learn about and explore. But her excitement faded away as she listened to the guest speaker, Edward Donleavy. Donleavy was a white man who talked about all the wonderful opportunities white students had at their high school and praised the black high school for producing top athletes.

"Lift Every Voice and Sing"

"Lift Every Voice and Sing" was originally a poem written by James Weldon Johnson in 1900. His brother, J. Rosamond Johnson, helped James turn it into a song. It expresses the strength many African Americans draw from the fact that their ancestors were slaves. The song is still sung in many schools today.

"Lift Every Voice and Sing"
by James Weldon Johnson

Lift ev'ry voice and sing,
'til earth and heaven ring,
Ring with the harmonies of Liberty;
Let our rejoicing rise
High as the list'ning skies,
Let it resound loud as the rolling sea.
Sing a song full of the faith that the dark past has taught us;
Sing a song full of the hope that the present has brought us
Facing the rising sun of our new day begun
Let us march on till victory is won.

It was at this moment that Marguerite really began to understand what it meant to be African-American in the United States in the 1940s. No matter how smart she was or how hard she worked, it seemed no one believed that African-American people could be successful and achieve great things. She was discouraged by Donleavy's speech, but her heart lifted at the end of graduation when "Lift Every Voice and Sing" was played. The song describes African Americans as strong people able to overcome any difficulties in life. Today, "Lift Every Voice and Sing" is still considered an important song in African-American **culture**.

After graduation, Momma decided it was time for Marguerite and Bailey to go back to live with their mother. She saved up the money for the train fare and traveled with Marguerite to Los Angeles, California, where Marguerite's mother was living. A month later, Bailey traveled to California, too.

Marguerite moved with her family to San Francisco around the time that the United States entered World War II. This photo shows the Nob Hill area in San Francisco in the early 1940s. The Mark Hopkins Hotel can be seen in the background of the photo.

Chapter 2:
Life in California

On Sunday December 7, 1941, several months after Marguerite and Bailey settled in with their mother, Japanese planes bombed the United States Navy base at Pearl Harbor in Hawaii. As a result, the United States became involved in World War II, a conflict which, up until then, had been fought mostly in Europe and Asia. The day of the bombing, Marguerite was on her way to the movies. When she heard people talking about the war, she ran all the way home, thinking she might be bombed before she got there.

Soon after the war began, Marguerite's mother married a man Marguerite called Daddy Clidell. To Marguerite, Daddy Clidell seemed like a real father, especially when he moved his new family into an apartment in San Francisco, California.

This is a page from the 1948 yearbook of the California Labor School in San Francisco, where Marguerite studied drama and dance.

Time for school

In 1941 Marguerite attended George Washington High School in San Francisco. She was quite surprised that she was not the best student there. Because she had been such a good reader for so long and her grades were very good in Stamps, she just naturally thought she would be better than anyone else. She was also uncomfortable being one of only three African-American students in the whole school. It was a good learning experience for Marguerite. She realized that even though she was a good reader, she had to study and work hard to get good grades.

In her second year in high school, Marguerite won a scholarship to the California Labor School. There, she studied dance and drama at night. Her mother thought that the school would help Marguerite get over her shyness. She soon found great enjoyment in the music and the beauty of the dance movements.

One summer, Marguerite went to visit her father who was living in Southern California. The visit was not as pleasant as she had hoped. Her father didn't seem to care that she was there and his new girlfriend was cruel. Disappointed and tired of being mistreated, Marguerite ran away. Not knowing where to go, she spent the night at a garbage dump. In the morning, she was surprised to find that many other children had spent the night there. For a month she lived among them, learning how to take care of herself. Finally she called her mother and asked her for a train ticket home.

This is the kind of streetcar Marguerite worked on in San Francisco in the 1940s.

Time for work

Life at home was not as happy for Marguerite as it should have been. Bailey, at age 16, was not getting along with his mother and decided to leave home. He had no idea where he was going, but he let Marguerite know that he could not stay. After Bailey left, Marguerite was so lonely that she felt she had to make a change.

At age 15, Marguerite decided she wanted to be a conductor on a San Francisco streetcar. She liked the uniforms the female conductors got to wear. Marguerite went to the railway office and asked for a job application. The secretaries in the office laughed at her and she went home in tears. In an interview, she remembered what happened next:

"My mother asked me, 'Why do you think they wouldn't give you an application?' I said, 'Because I'm [black].' She asked, 'Do you want the job?' I said, 'Yes.' She said, 'Go get it! I will give you money. Every morning you get down there before the secretaries are there. Take yourself a good book. Now, when lunchtime comes, don't leave until they leave. But when they leave, you go and give yourself a good lunch. But be back before the secretaries, if you really want that job.'"

For three weeks Marguerite waited in the office for an application. The secretaries purposely bumped into her as they walked past and called her names, trying to make her go home. Finally, they gave her an application. She filled it out, and within a month she got the job. Marguerite became the first African-American streetcar conductor in San Francisco. She spent six months clanking up and down the city streets.

After about six months of work, Marguerite decided she was tired of her job. She went back to high school, but it was not the same. She felt much older than the other students. School bored her, and she cut classes. She took long walks in the park or wandered around the department stores. When her mother found out what she was doing, she told Marguerite to make up her mind. She was either going to go to school or she had to quit. Marguerite chose to return to George Washington High School.

When Marguerite graduated in August 1945, she was pregnant. She had been involved in a relationship with a boy from her neighborhood. A few months later her son, Clyde Johnson, was born. Marguerite was only seventeen years old. Her mother and Daddy Clidell wanted to take care of Clyde so Marguerite could go to college, but Marguerite wanted to try to make it on her own.

After renting a room and hiring a babysitter, Marguerite took just about any job she could find. She worked as a cook at a restaurant, but soon realized that the life of a cook was not the life for her. Taking Clyde with her, she moved to San Diego and became a waitress in a nightclub. Her life was lonely and difficult, but she still had her books. She became interested in great Russian writers like Leo Tolstoy and the **playwright** Maxim Gorky. But nothing helped her loneliness, so she decided to go home. This time, "home" meant Stamps, Arkansas, and Momma.

Marguerite loved to read. Among her favorite authors was Lee Tolstoy, pictured above. Tolstoy is perhaps best known for his book War and Peace.

Unfortunately, Stamps was just as **racist** a town as Marguerite remembered. It was good to see Momma again, but Marguerite knew she could not stay in a town filled with so much **prejudice**. A few months after they arrived, she and Clyde were on their way back to San Francisco.

Maya Angelou began her performing career in the 1950s. She is shown here in a photo from a play she appeared in called Calypso Heatwave.

Chapter 3: On Stage

Back in San Francisco Marguerite took two part-time jobs that did not pay much. She was also raising her three-year-old son on her own. What little free time she had she spent at a local record store. She couldn't afford to buy anything, but listening to the music was free. The music made her feel happy and helped her forget her troubles for a while. The store owner noticed how much Marguerite enjoyed music and offered her a job working in the store. Since the job paid more than her part-time work, Marguerite happily accepted.

One day while Marguerite was working, a sailor walked into the record store. He began talking to Marguerite about jazz, an exciting style of music that is played by musicians who often make up rhythms, melodies, and beats as they play. The sailor's name was Tosh Angelos, and he was soon coming into the store every day to see Marguerite.

Since Tosh was white, it was hard for Marguerite to imagine dating him. What would people think? When she wrote to Bailey about Tosh, he told her not to worry about what other people thought and to do what she thought was right. Tosh and Marguerite were married in 1952.

Marguerite quit her job at the record store and became a housewife. She felt safe and wanted, and life seemed good. But Marguerite was lonely. Tosh didn't like her friends, so he wouldn't allow them to visit. He didn't believe in God, so he wouldn't allow Marguerite to go to church. There was no one in her life but Clyde and Tosh. And then Tosh was gone, too. A year after they were married, Tosh decided that he didn't want to be married anymore.

Before they separated, Marguerite had an operation that kept her in the hospital for a few weeks. While she was still recovering, she learned that Momma had died. Missing Momma's funeral made Marguerite feel awful. It took her a very long time to get over the sadness.

On her own

Now that Marguerite was separated, she needed to find a job. Despite the fact that she had never performed before, except at her drama school, and had very little training, she got a job as a dancer at a nightclub. She did so well that she was hired at another nightclub in San Francisco called the Purple Onion.

This photo shows the entrance to the Purple Onion nightclub in San Francisco, where Maya Angelou once performed. The club still hosts comedy acts and other types of shows today.

To dance at the Purple Onion, Marguerite needed an exciting new name. Marguerite was too long, and "Rita" did not seem mysterious enough. She decided to use the name Bailey always called her—Maya. The club owners liked that, but she needed a last name as well. She decided to use Angelos, which was Tosh's last name. The owners dropped the *s*, added a *u*, and pronounced it *an-gell-oo*. She was now Maya Angelou.

Maya soon became so well known at the club that she was invited to perform on local television shows. People began to recognize her on the street. She was becoming part of a new world of African-American artists, dancers, singers, actors, and performers. For the first time, her creative life and her working life overlapped.

Then, in 1953, something even more thrilling happened. Broadway was (and still is) an area of theaters in New York City where some of the best musicals and plays in the world are performed. A popular Broadway show called *New Faces of 1953* came to San Francisco and Maya was offered a part in the production. She had to turn it down because she couldn't get the time off. When she was offered a part in *Porgy and Bess*, an all-black **opera** by American composer George Gershwin, she went to a performance. She fell in love with the beautiful music and the gorgeous costumes.

This picture is a stage shot from a production of Porgy and Bess. *Angelou traveled to countries in Europe and Africa playing the character Ruby in the opera in 1954.*

The cast of *Porgy and Bess* went to see Maya perform at the Purple Onion. They wanted her to join them when the show went to perform in Europe for a year. Maya knew she could not go. She still had three months left with the Purple Onion. Taking the job would also mean leaving Clyde at home.

When her work at the Purple Onion was up, *Porgy and Bess* had not yet left for Europe. Maya very much wanted to perform in the show. Her mother agreed to take care of Clyde, so Maya went to Europe.

On tour

Porgy and Bess played to sold-out audiences in 22 nations of Europe and Africa. Everywhere Maya went, she took a grammar book with her. She learned the languages of different countries quickly, including French, Spanish, Italian, and Arabic. She was especially excited when the company toured countries in Africa. Everywhere they performed, the all-African-American group was greeted by cheering audiences.

Even though Maya was happy touring in *Porgy and Bess*, she felt sad about leaving her son at home. She thought of him daily and wondered if she had made the right decision. She received a letter from her mother who was about to start working in a casino in Las Vegas, Nevada. She would not be able to take care of Clyde.

Porgy and Bess

The story of Porgy and Bess is based on a real-life story of a handicapped African-American man who committed murder. The **opera** takes place in Catfish Row, which once was a mansion but became a crowded waterfront apartment building in Charleston, South Carolina.

In 1926 George Gershwin, a famous composer of musicals, read the novel *Porgy* by DuBose Heyward. Gershwin suggested that he and Heyward work together to create a "folk opera" based on the story. In 1934 Heyward, Gershwin, and Gershwin's brother Ira finally got together to write the opera. It was finished in 1935. Today the opera is well-loved, but it was not successful in the United States during Gershwin's lifetime. It was much more popular in Europe. Today Gershwin and Heyward are respected in part for their sensitive and respectful treatment of African-American **culture**.

The songs "Summertime" and "I Got Plenty o' Nuttin'" are two of the best-known songs from *Porgy and Bess.*

Angelou's son, Guy, is shown in this photo as a young man.

Maya's mother also wrote that Clyde had developed a rash on his body, that doctors could not cure. Maya knew it was time to go home.

Maya returned to California in 1955 to find her nine-year-old son had become quiet and withdrawn. Her first night home, Clyde asked where she was going next. Maya told him she would never leave him again. Soon after her return, Clyde's rash cleared up, and he was acting like his old self again. He also announced that he wanted to be called Guy because "Clyde" sounded "too mushy."

A few months later, Maya received a telegram offering her a job singing for four weeks at a hotel in Hawaii. The offer included transportation for both her and Guy, so they decided to go together. When they got to Hawaii, Guy was the first to notice the huge sign in front of the hotel. It said "MAYA ANGELOU" in large letters. Guy proudly told a waiter at a hotel restaurant that the sign was for his mother.

After four weeks, Maya and Clyde returned to California. In Hawaii she developed a singing and dancing act that she could perform anywhere, so she took it on the road. In the late 1950s, she and Guy moved to New York City. There, she performed in a couple of plays and recorded a record.

James Baldwin (1924–1987)

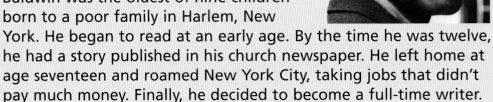

James Arthur Baldwin was a good friend of Maya Angelou's. He encouraged her to write her **autobiography,** which helped to establish her as a writer. Baldwin was also a talented novelist, **playwright,** and essayist. He was an important author in the late 1950s and early 1960s.

Baldwin was the oldest of nine children born to a poor family in Harlem, New York. He began to read at an early age. By the time he was twelve, he had a story published in his church newspaper. He left home at age seventeen and roamed New York City, taking jobs that didn't pay much money. Finally, he decided to become a full-time writer.

After living in Europe for ten years, Baldwin published his first novel, *Go Tell It On the Mountain* (1953). It told about his experiences as a teenage preacher in a small church.

In 1957 Baldwin returned to the United States and became involved in the **civil rights** struggle. He wrote about feelings about African-American and white relations in the United States in his book *Nobody Knows My Name* (1961). His book *The Fire Next Time* (1963) warned white Americans of violence unless they changed their racist attitudes.

In 1974 Baldwin shifted away from political writing and wrote *If Beale Street Could Talk*, a moving love story. He then wrote a number of short stories and novels. His last work was *The Price of the Ticket* in 1985, a collection of autobiographical writings. Baldwin continued to write until he died of cancer in France in 1987.

In the 1950s and 1960s, New York was a city full of creative energy. In a neighborhood called Harlem, African-American writers, artists, and performers were speaking out about about **racism** and **injustice**. They used their art to express their political beliefs. Maya joined the Harlem Writers Guild, where she met famous African-American writers like James Baldwin. At the Guild's weekly meetings, she learned that writing takes hard work and discipline. She also began to take a real interest in politics.

African-American musicians such as Louis Armstrong, Duke Ellington, and Cab Calloway performed at the Cotton Club in Harlem, New York.

Chapter 4:
Fighting for Civil Rights

The late 1950s and 1960s were a time of great change in the United States. The writers and artists in Harlem had become more and more political as a result of the growing **civil rights** movement. The movement had begun in the southern United States. The South was much more racially **segregated** than other parts of the country, and leaders like Dr. Martin Luther King Jr. were trying to bring segregation to an end. In 1957 King helped create an organization called the Southern Christian Leadership Conference (SCLC). SCLC was a group of people who worked hard to make sure African Americans all over the United States were treated fairly and given the rights they deserved. SCLC had branches all over the country.

In the late 1950s Maya heard Dr. King give a speech about **racism** in the United States. The speech inspired her to write a show called Freedom Cabaret. Freedom Cabaret was a combination of musical and dramatic pieces performed by different African-American artists. Maya hoped the show would raise money for the SCLC.

A new family

In 1959 Maya was surprised to get a call from Bayard Rustin, the coordinator of the SCLC in the northern states. He was leaving the SCLC and wanted her to replace him. Maya had never been involved with such work before, but Rustin thought she would be good at leading the organization. From 1961–1962, Maya was the northern coordinator of the SCLC.

During that time, Maya met Vusumzi Make, a black lawyer from South Africa. At the time, black South Africans were living under a system of racial **segregation** called apartheid. Because he dared to speak out and say that apartheid was wrong, Make's life was in danger. He fled to United States for safety. Maya liked his ideas and his manners, and Guy liked him, too. Make and Maya were married in early 1961.

A short time later, Make announced that he thought the family would be happier in Africa. They would all be moving to Cairo, Egypt. Maya looked forward to a new life in northern Africa.

Bayard Rustin, the man who recommended Angelou for a job with the Southern Christian Leadership Conference, is seen here on the right. He is shown speaking to U.S. senators in 1966, along with union leader A. Phillip Randolph.

Life in Africa

Guy enjoyed his new home and learned Arabic—the main language spoken in Egypt—very quickly. Although Make did not want Maya to work, she got a job with the *Arab Observer*, an English-language newspaper. She wrote news stories and **editorials**, and sometimes read them on the air for the radio station Radio Cairo.

By 1963, Maya's marriage to Make was over. She and Guy moved to Accra, a city in Ghana, Africa. Two days after they arrived, Guy was in a car accident and nearly died. While Guy recovered, Maya reconnected with Julian Mayfield, an old friend from the Harlem Writers Guild. Mayfield was living in Ghana and helped Maya get a job at a local university. When Guy was well enough, he enrolled at the university and moved on campus.

Maya was happy in Ghana. Living in a country where black people were the majority and ran the government was very exciting. But Ghana was not home. Maya was concerned about what was happening with the **civil rights movement** in the United States. She and other African Americans living in Accra listened to the radio for news. According to the reports, there were riots in many cities across the United States. Hundreds of African Americans and other Americans had been thrown in jail. Martin Luther King Jr. was in jail in Birmingham, Alabama, for leading a nonviolent protest. Police officers patrolled the streets of Birmingham with police dogs, trying to keep order.

This photo of Angelou was taken while she lived in Cairo, Egypt.

*Martin Luther King Jr. delivered his famous "I Have a Dream" speech at the March on Washington in August 1963. African Americans who traveled to the march from around the country faced serious threats to their safety from **racist** groups.*

Then came news of a huge march in Washington, D.C., that Dr. King was planning for the summer of 1963. He hoped to gather a crowd of people too large for the United States government to ignore. He hoped to finally get the government to pass new laws that would end segregation.

On August 28, 1963, about 250,000 people gathered in Washington, D.C., for what came to be known as the March on Washington. Dr. King delivered his famous "I Have a Dream" speech.

Maya and her friends decided to stage a similar march on the United States **embassy** in Accra. They carried torches to the embassy at night. As the marchers waited until dawn, two U.S. Marines came out of the embassy to raise the American flag that flew in front of the building. One Marine was black. Maya and the others called for him to join their protest, but he refused.

A few months later, Maya left Ghana to perform in a show. She spent several months touring Europe before returning to Africa. She knew that Guy no longer needed her as much as he had when he was younger. She left him to finish school and made plans to return to the United States.

*Angelou met and talked with the **activist** Malcolm X in Ghana in 1963, shortly before he was killed.*

Chapter 5:
The Writer

While in Africa, Maya Angelou met Malcolm X, a powerful black leader who was also part of the American **civil rights** movement. Unlike Dr. King, however, who believed that nonviolent protests and marches were the best way for African Americans to gain the rights they deserved, Malcolm X believed that African Americans should do anything they could to secure their rights, even if it meant using violence. In 1964, Angelou returned to America to work with Malcolm X. But first she wanted to visit her mother and her brother Bailey in San Francisco.

Shortly after arriving in San Francisco, Angelou learned from a friend that Malcolm X had been killed. He'd been shot to death by people who did not agree with him. Angelou was extremely upset, and to help her take her mind off of her pain, Bailey arranged for her to sing in a nightclub in Hawaii. Soon after she started, however, Angelou left the nightclub and moved to Los Angeles.

This photo shows three stores that were set on fire during the Watts riots on August 13, 1965, in Los Angeles, California.

While in Los Angeles, Angelou worked in a poor, mostly-African-American neighborhood called Watts. The people living there were frustrated. They were tired of living in such a neglected neighborhood. They wanted more jobs, better schools, and better places to live. On August 11, 1965, the people of Watts exploded in anger. What began as a protest against the way an African-American man had been treated by a police officer grew into one of the worst riots in United States history. Stores were looted and burned, and more than 30 people died. Angelou was shocked by the amount of violence and destruction, but she was not surprised that the people of Watts were so angry.

The Watts Riots

Tensions between African Americans and other Americans in American cities had been growing for many years. To help ease these tensions, the United States government passed the **Civil Rights** Act of 1964. The act was supposed to protect the rights of African Americans and help improve the relationships between African Americans and white Americans. One part of the act promised to improve the living conditions of African Americans living in cities, but some states, including California, passed laws that blocked the better housing part of the Civil Rights Act.

On August 11, 1965, in Watts, a Los Angeles, California neighborhood, a police officer pulled over an African-American man named Marquette Frye for driving drunk. A crowd gathered to see what was happening and eventually a fight broke out. The police tried to break up the fight with their batons. This made the crowd extremely angry. After the police left the scene with Frye, the crowd began a riot that lasted for six days. About 1,000 people were injured and more than 30 people died. The damage to property was said to be almost $100 million.

After the riots, government officials realized that the rioters were people who had been pushed to the breaking point. They were fed up with the poverty and joblessness in their neighborhood. They wanted the better living conditions that were promised them in the Civil Rights Act. Unfortunately, little was done to help the people of Watts after the riots, and no real effort was made to rebuild the parts of the community that had been destroyed. Today, however, Watts is a thriving community working to get past the **racial** tensions that lead to the 1965 riots.

These volunteers from the organization Habitat for Humanity built a house together in the Watts neighborhood in Los Angeles, California.

For most of her 40 years, Angelou had been on the move, from city to city, country to country. She now considered moving to New York, and Bailey encouraged her to go. While in New York, Angelou renewed her friendship with author James Baldwin. He often listened to her telling stories of her life in Stamps, Arkansas. She kept him and others people entertained for hours with her quiet retelling of things both sad and funny. Baldwin wanted her to write her stories down just the way she told them. She wasn't interested.

After some thought, Angelou changed her mind and sat down to write. What she wrote became her first book called *I Know Why the Caged Bird Sings*, published in 1970. She dedicated the book to her son Guy. She took the title from a poem called "Sympathy" by African-American poet Paul Laurence Dunbar. The poem is about how much people who are not free long for their freedom.

I Know Why the Caged Bird Sings was a great success for Angelou. Critics called her a genius for her poetic use of language. They said she expressed herself with courage and dignity. *I Know Why the Caged Bird Sings* was nominated for a National Book Award. National Book Awards are given each year to exceptional books written by Americans.

Angelou is shown here with a copy of her first book, I Know Why the Caged Bird Sings.

An outpouring of work

After *I Know Why the Caged Bird Sings* was published, the number of artistic works Angelou produced was amazing. In 1971 she published a book of poetry called *Just Give Me a Cool Drink of Water 'fore I Die.* The book was nominated for a **Pulitzer Prize**, the highest prize awarded to a work of literature in the United States. In 1972, Angelou became the first African-American woman to produce a **screenplay**.

She published the next three volumes of her **autobiography** in little more than ten years. *Gather Together in My Name* (1974) begins at the end of World War II (1939–1945) when Angelou graduated from high school. *Singin' and Swingin' and Gettin' Merry Like Christmas* (1976) tells of her marriage to Make and her journey to Africa. *The Heart of a Woman* (1981) covers the **civil rights** movement and changes in both Africa and the United States. The fifth volume, *All God's Children Need Traveling Shoes*, was published in 1986. It covers her life in Africa and ends with her decision to return home. The sixth book, *A Song Flung Up to Heaven* (2002), begins with her return from Africa and the death of Malcolm X. It ends with her getting ready to write her first autobiography.

In 1977, one of television's most popular miniseries was *Roots*, a show based on a book by Alex Haley. It told the story of slaves taken out of Africa and their treatment in America. Angelou was nominated for an **Emmy Award** for playing the grandmother of Kunta Kinte, the series' main character. Angelou also wrote the words and music for the television movie version of *I Know Why the Caged Bird Sings*, which aired in 1979.

In 1993, Maya Angelou appeared in the film Poetic Justice along with costars Janet Jackson and Tupac Shakur. She also wrote poetry that was featured in the film.

Chapter 6:
All About Survival

Over the next decades, Angelou continued to use and develop her many talents. Acting, writing, producing, directing—she did it all. It seemed impossible that Angelou had the time and energy to do so much. Her play *Sister, Sister*, about a middle-class African-American family, was shown on NBC television in 1982. She appeared in John Singleton's film *Poetic Justice* in 1993, and also wrote poetry for the film. She published two books of essays that same year, *Lessons in Life* and *Wouldn't Take Nothing for My Journey Now*. She also found time to write books for children. Among them is *My Painted House, My Friendly Chicken, and Me*, a book about a girl in South Africa. Her book of poetry for children, *Life Doesn't Frighten Me*, helps children learn to deal with their fears.

In 1993, Angelou read a poem she had written especially for the occasion at U.S. President Bill Clinton's inauguration. She initially had trouble completing the poem, "On the Pulse of the Morning," but finished it the week before the inauguration.

The inauguration

Maya Angelou's fame became widespread the morning of January 20, 1993. William Jefferson Clinton was being **inaugurated** as the 42nd president of the United States. Clinton asked Angelou to read one of her poems at the ceremony in Washington, D.C. She was only the second poet in U.S. history to read an original piece of writing at an inauguration. The whole country watched as Angelou read a poem she wrote specifically for the occasion. It was called "On the Pulse of Morning" and was about the hope that Angelou had for the United States. The Clintons were so impressed that they hung a copy of the poem in the White House. Angelou would later win a **Grammy Award** for her recording of the poem.

Although Angelou is a public figure, she is a very private person. She does not spend as much time at home as she would like to because of her lecturing schedule. Angelou gives about 80 lectures a year.

Even when she is at home, she does not write there. She prefers to go to a motel so she will not be distracted. She gets up at five o'clock in the morning and gathers her dictionary, pencils, and a yellow legal pad. She works at the motel until early afternoon, or sometimes into the evening. Then she goes back home for the night. She continues this routine until the poem or book she is working on is finished.

In 2004, Angelou published a cookbook called *Hallelujah! The Welcome Table* full of recipes and memories from her childhood. Every picture in the book is of a dish Angelou cooked herself. For ten days straight she baked and stirred, recreating from memory the dishes her mother and Momma made. Neither of them ever wrote a single recipe down.

Maya Angelou overcame many obstacles to achieve the great success she enjoys today. She battled **racism**, struggled through poverty, and survived abuse. She has seen the United States go through great changes and is still fighting to make the United States the best nation it can be. Angelou is a mother, **activist**, and **documentarian**. But most of all, she is a writer. "That's what I do," she once said in an interview. "That's how I describe myself to myself. . . . And if I think God has forgotten my name, I'll ask him, 'Remember me? The Writer?'"

Angelou is shown here in a photo from 1998. In 1998, the film Down in the Delta *was released. It was the first film that Angelou directed.*

Glossary

activist person who believes in taking forceful action for political purposes

autobiography book written by a person about his or her life

civil rights rights of all United States citizens to fair and equal treatment under the law. The civil rights movement was the name given to the long fight to gain civil rights for African Americans.

culture beliefs and traditions of a specific group

discrimination treatment of some people better than others without a proper or fair reason

documentarian person who records factual information about a subject

embassy place in one country where representatives from other countries work and sometimes live

Emmy Award award given annually for the best performances in television

Grammy Award award given annually for the best performances in music

immigrant person who moves to a new country to live there

inauguration introduction into an office with suitable ceremonies

injustice unfairness or violation of the rights of another

opera musical stage production in which the story is sung

playwright person who writes plays

prejudice favoring or dislike of something for no good or fair reason

Pulitzer Prize prize given yearly for the best in journalism, creative writing, and music

racism belief that people of different races are not as good or equal as others. A racist is a person who practices racism.

screenplay written version of a story prepared for film production

segregated divided by race

Timeline

1928   Marguerite Annie Johnson (Maya Angelou) is born on April 4 in St. Louis, Missouri.

1942   Becomes first African-American streetcar conductor in San Francisco. Returns to high school after six months of work.

1945   Graduates from George Washington High School and gives birth to her son, Clyde Johnson.

1952   Marries first husband, Tosh Angelos.

1953–1955 Separates from husband and takes job as dancer at the Purple Onion nightclub. Gets part in all-black production of *Porgy and Bess* and tours Europe and Africa. Takes stage name of Maya Angelou.

1961   Angelou marries Vusumzi Make and moves to Cairo, Egypt.

1963   Moves to Accra, Ghana.

1970   Publishes first book, *I Know Why the Caged Bird Sings*.

1971   Is nominated for the Pulitzer Prize for *Just Give Me a Cool Drink of Water 'fore I Die.*

1974   Is nominated for an **Emmy Award** for role in *Roots.*

1982   Angelou's play *Sister Sister* airs on television.

1993   Recites her poem "On the Pulse of Morning" at **inauguration** of Bill Clinton. Appears in and writes poetry for *Poetic Justice* and publishes *Lessons in Life* and *Wouldn't Take Nothing for My Journey Now.*

1994   Wins **Grammy Award** for recording of inauguration poem and publishes *The Collected Poems of Maya Angelou.*

2002   Publishes *A Song Flung Up to Heaven.*

Further Information

Further reading

Gombos, Adrienne. *Equality Now: Tales of Women's Inequality.*
    Long Island City, N.J.: Star Bright, 2003.

Lisandrelli, Elaine Slivinski. *Maya Angelou: More Than a Poet.*
    Berkeley Heights, N.J.: Enslow Publishers, 1996.

Pettit, Jayne. *Maya Angelou: Journey of the Heart.*
    New York: Penguin, 1998.

Shuker, Nancy. *Maya Angelou: America's Poetic Voice.*
    Detroit: Gale Group, 2001.

Addresses

Maya Angelou
c/o Lordly & Dame, Inc.
Strategic Events International
51 Church St.
Boston, MA 02116

The Academy of American Poets
588 Broadway, Suite 604
New York, NY 10012-3210

PEN American Center
568 Broadway
New York, NY 10012

Index